COLORING

PEN CONTROL

TRACING

COUNTING

PRACTICE WORKBOOK

one whale

two slides

three elephants

four houses

five cars

six flowers

seven ducks

eight turtles

nine apples

ten lemons

eleven pencils

COLORING NUMBER 0-9

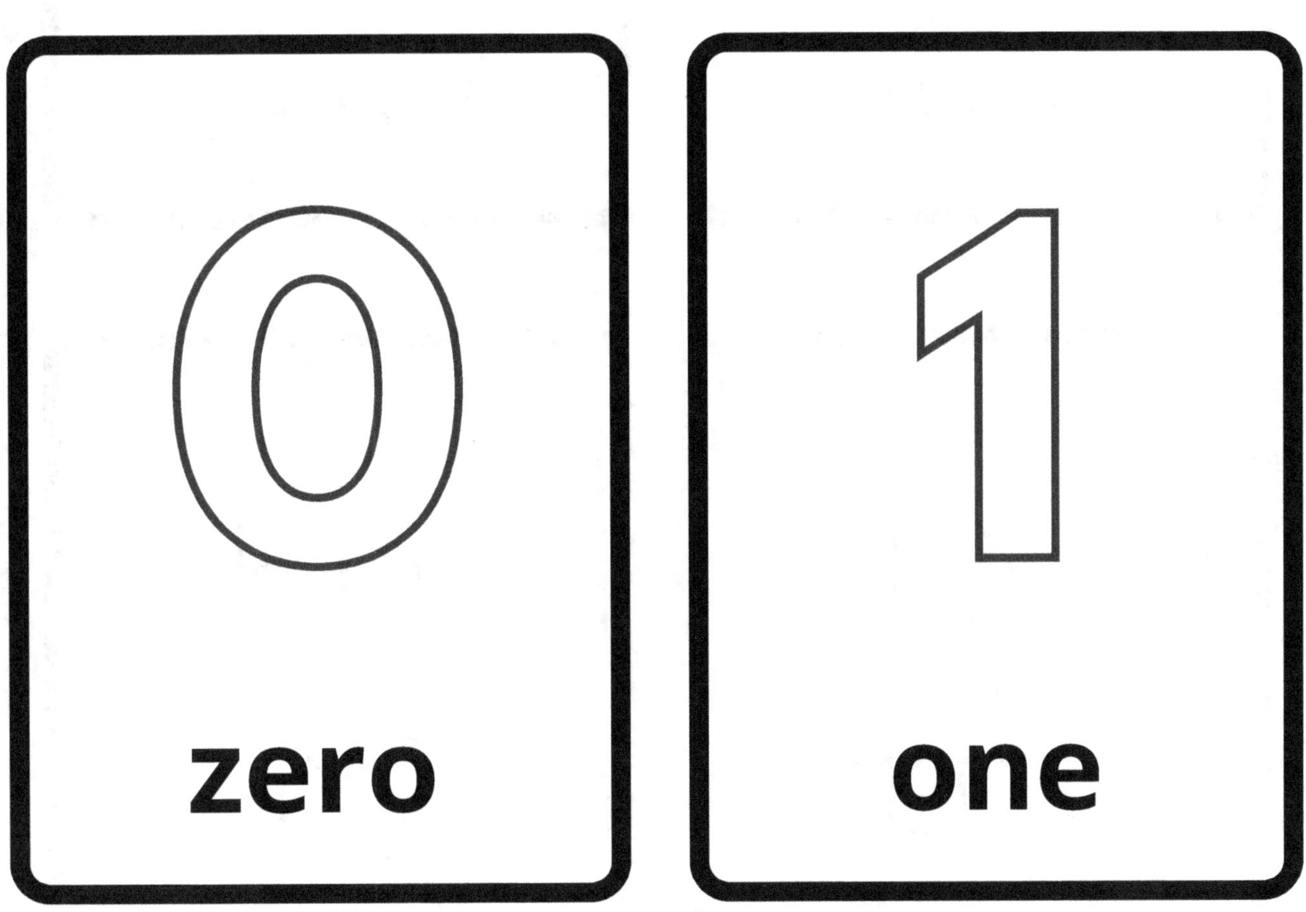

4
four

six

seven

eight

nine

TRACE THE NUMBERS
0-9

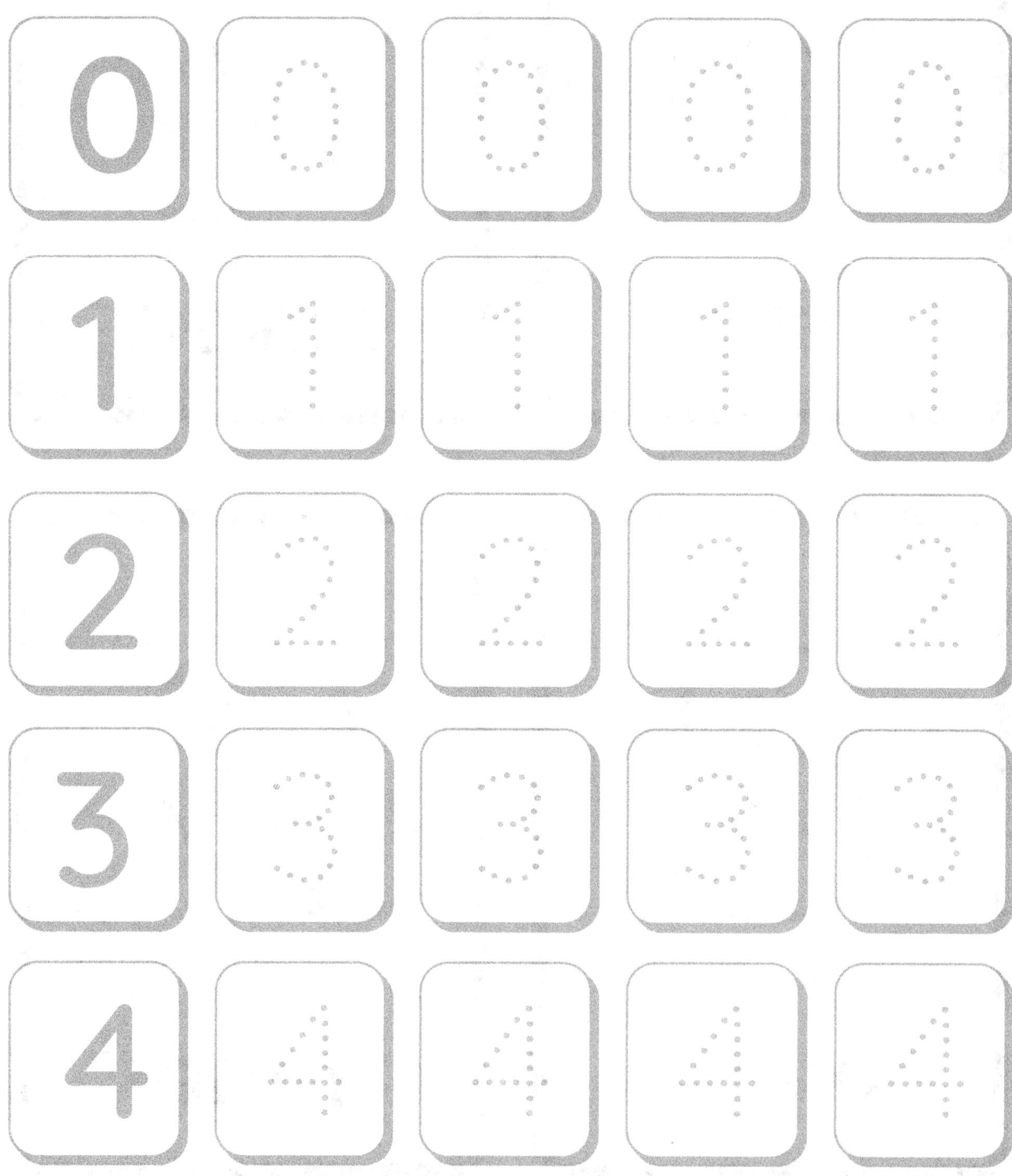

5	5	5	5	5
6	6	6	6	6
7	7	7	7	7
8	8	8	8	8
9	9	9	9	9

COUNT AND TRACE

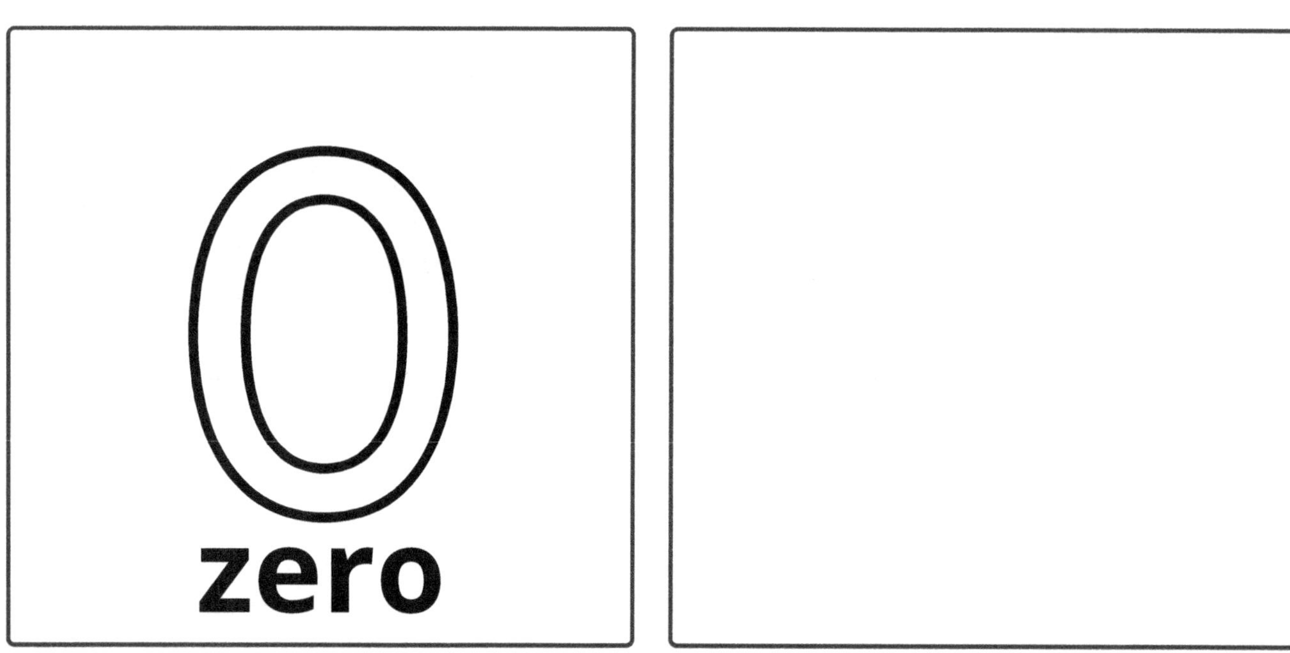

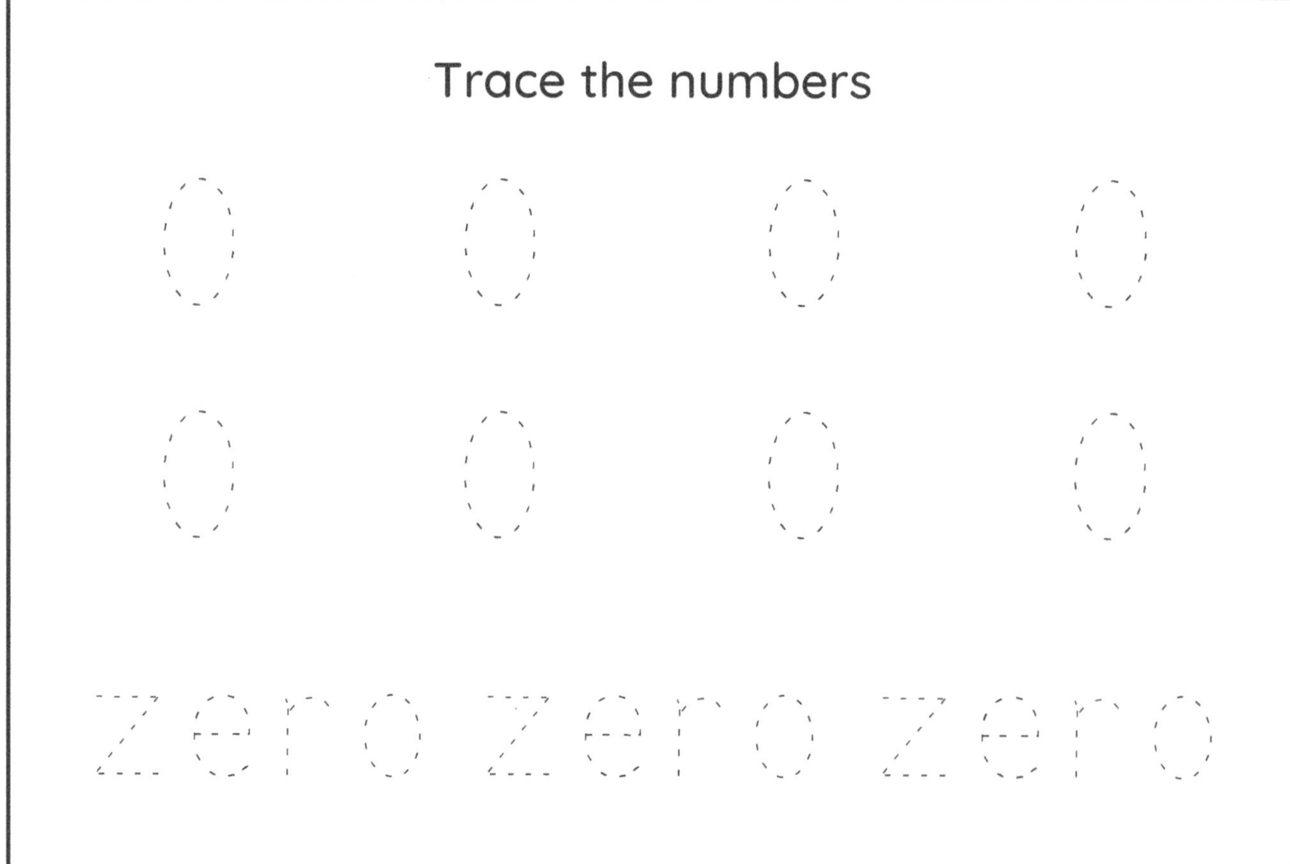

COUNT AND TRACE

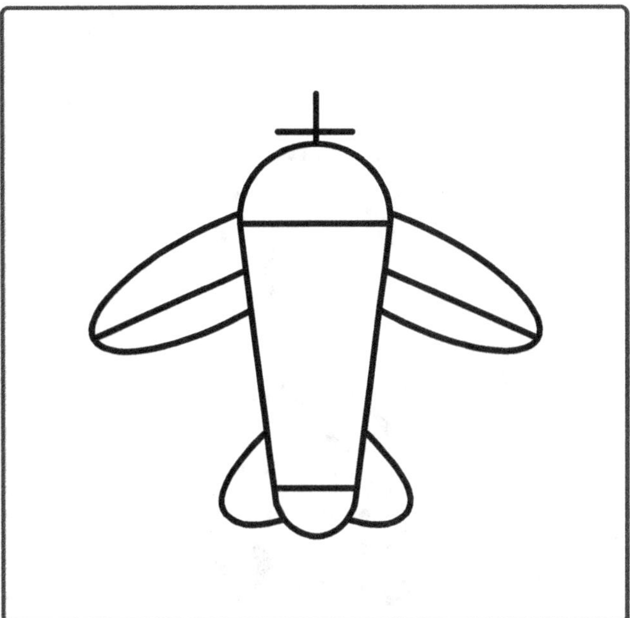

Trace the numbers

1 1 1 1

1 1 1 1

one one one

COUNT AND TRACE

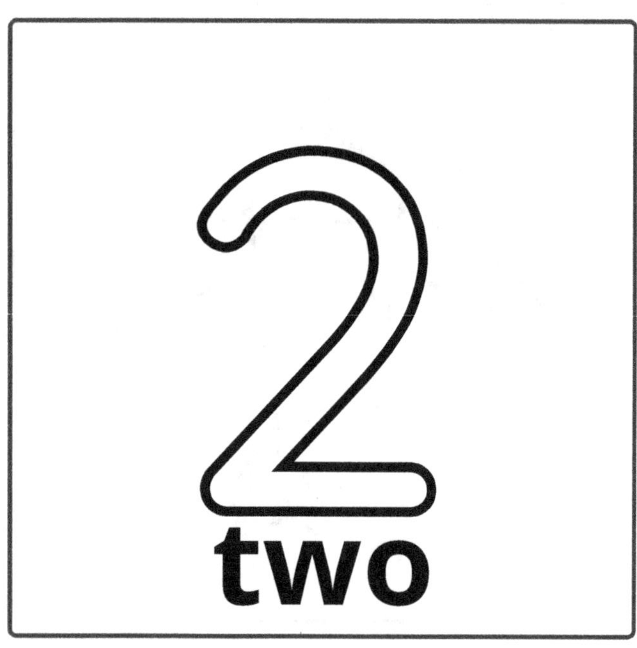

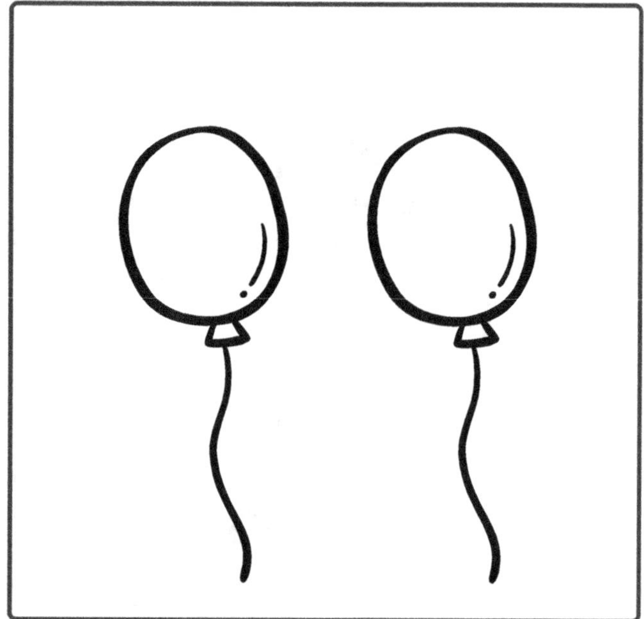

Trace the numbers

2 2 2 2

2 2 2 2

two two two

COUNT AND TRACE

Trace the numbers

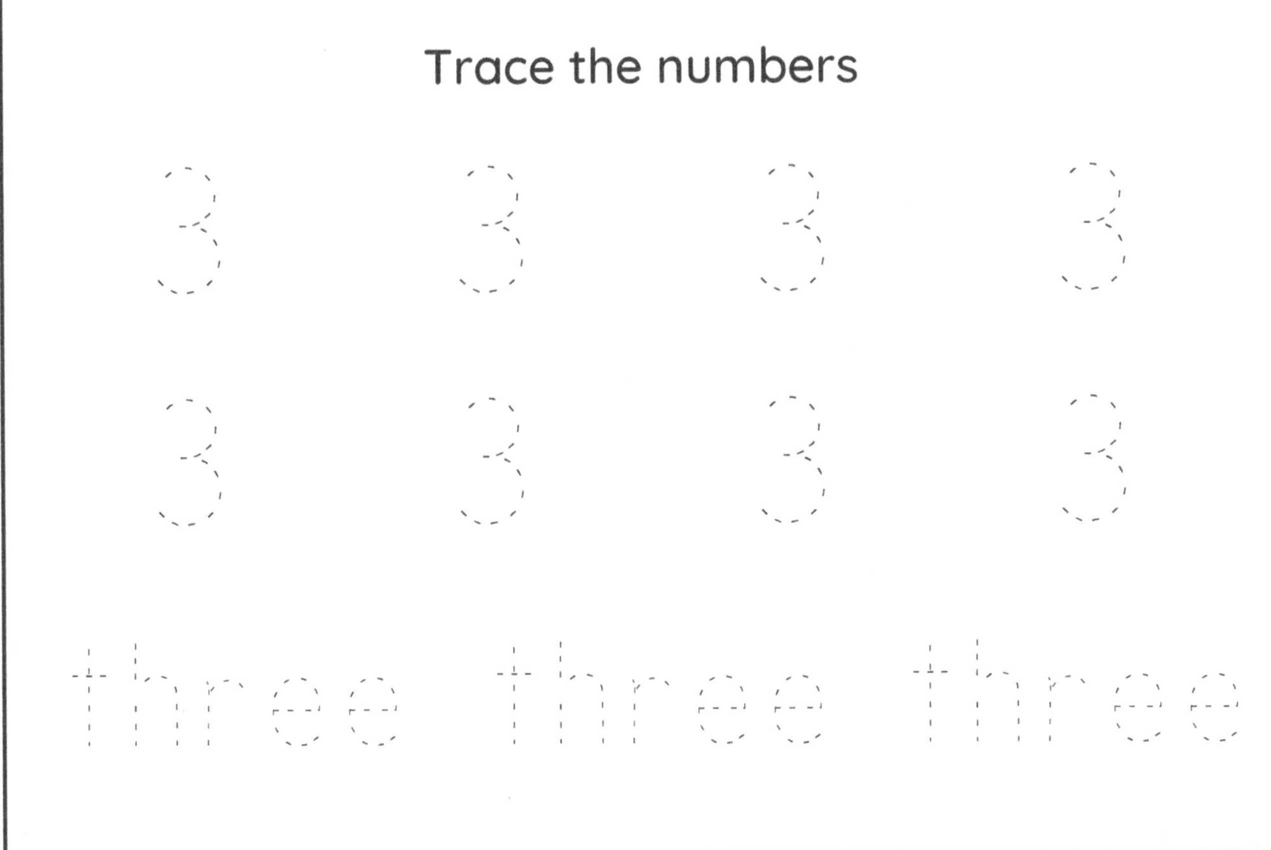

COUNT AND TRACE

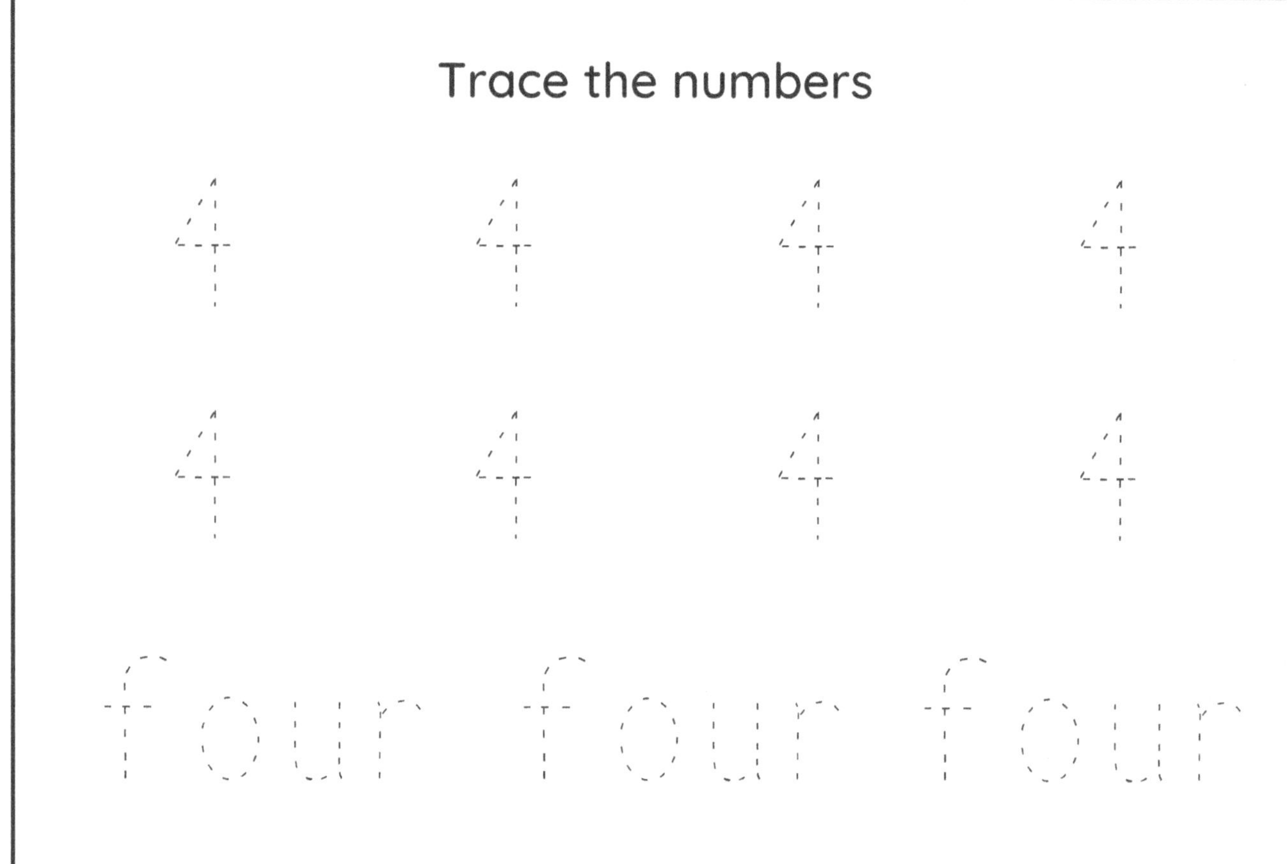

Trace the numbers

COUNT AND TRACE

Trace the numbers

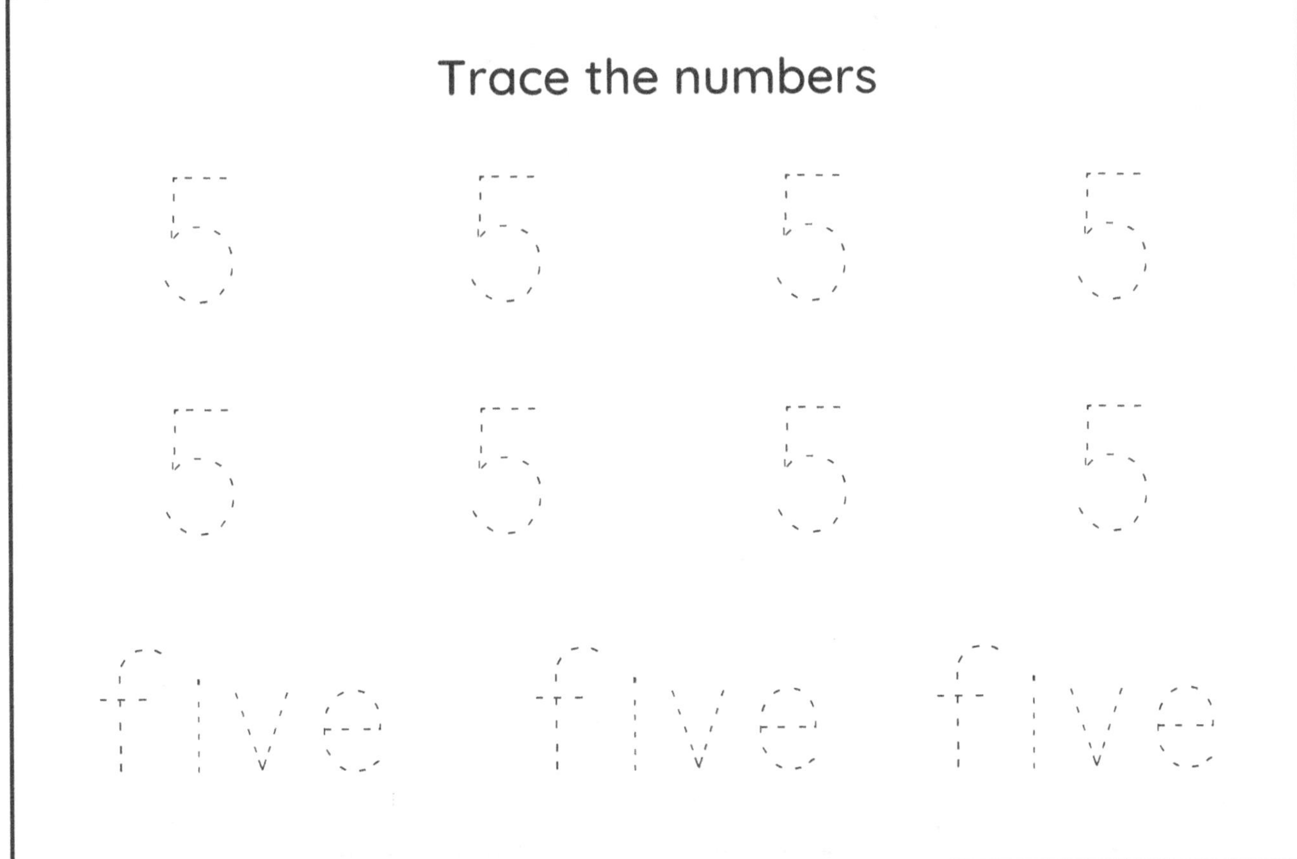

COUNT **AND** TRACE

Trace the numbers

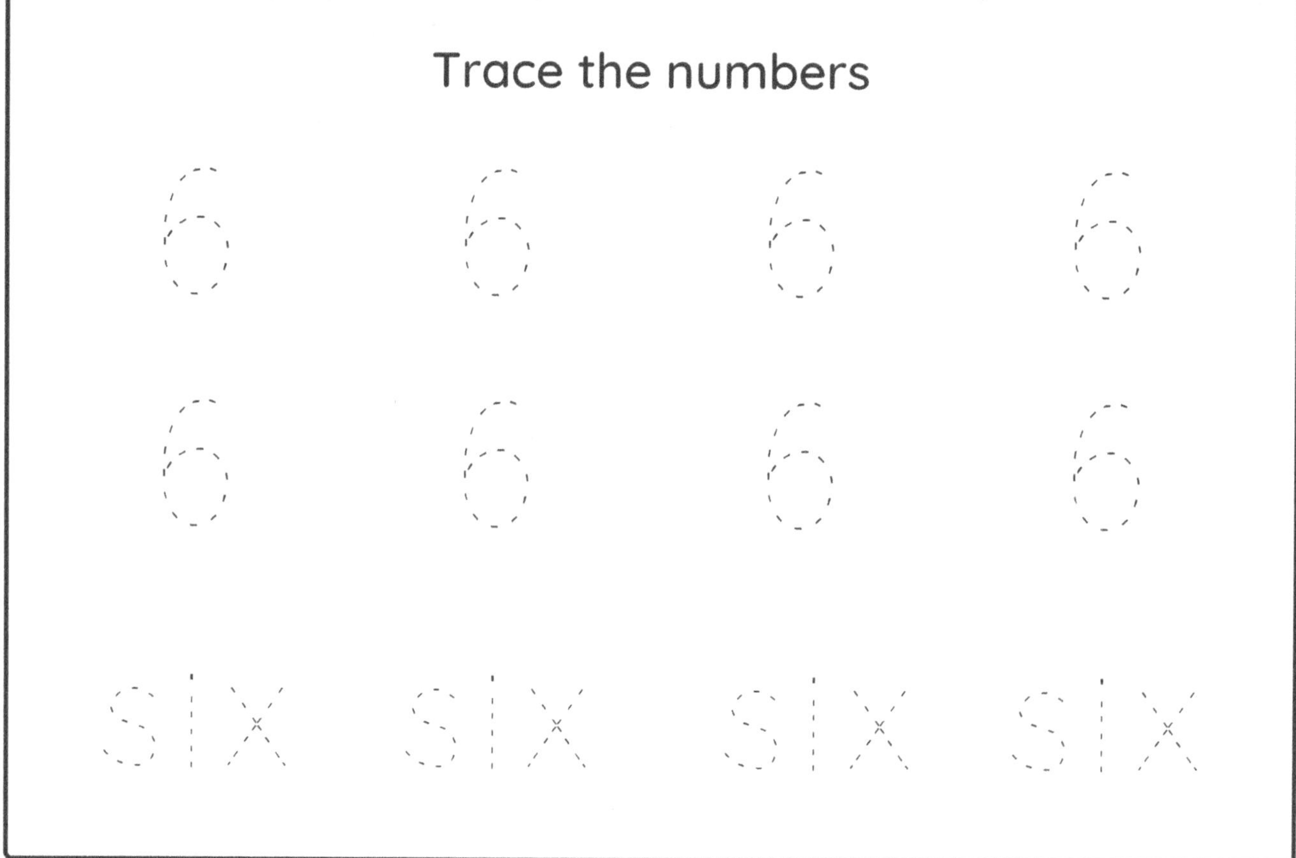

COUNT AND TRACE

Trace the numbers

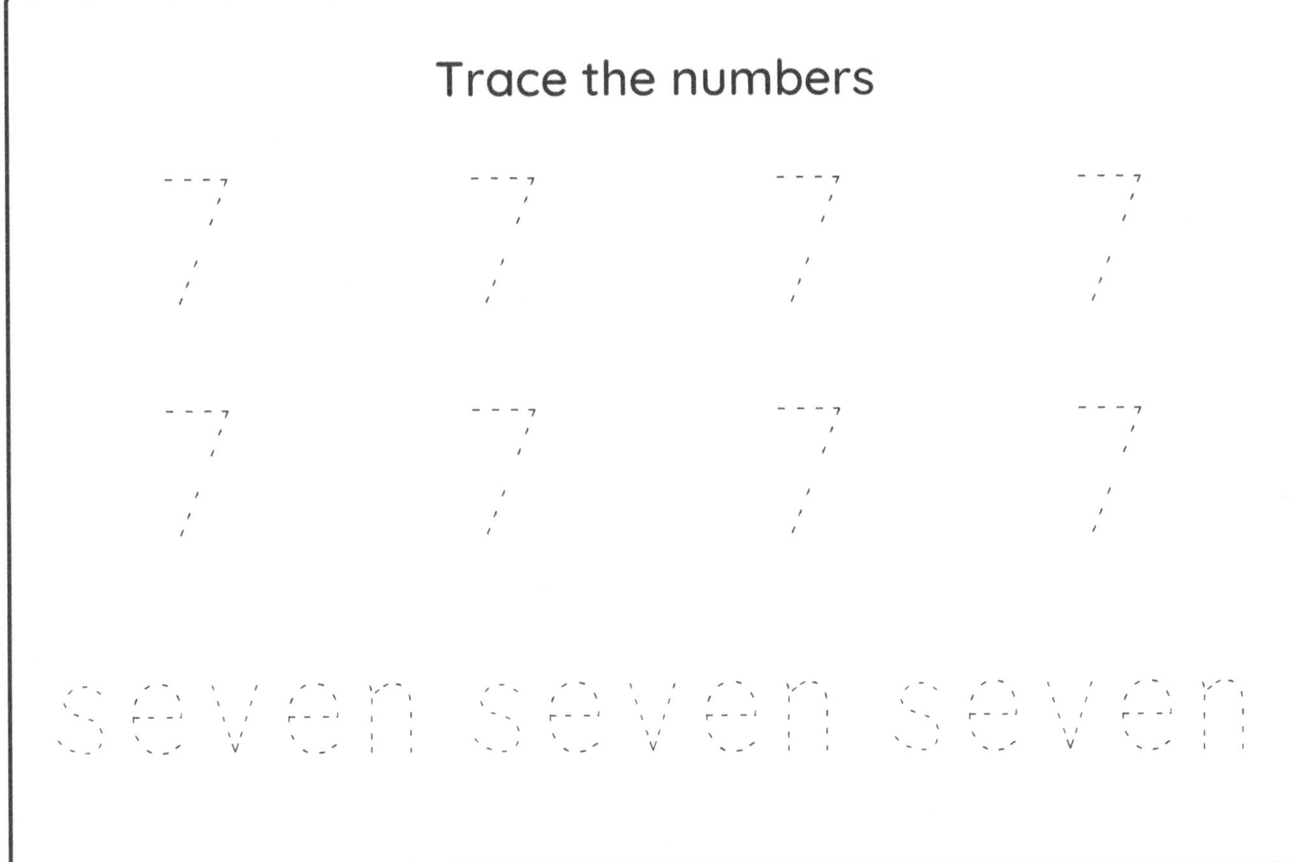

COUNT AND TRACE

8

eight

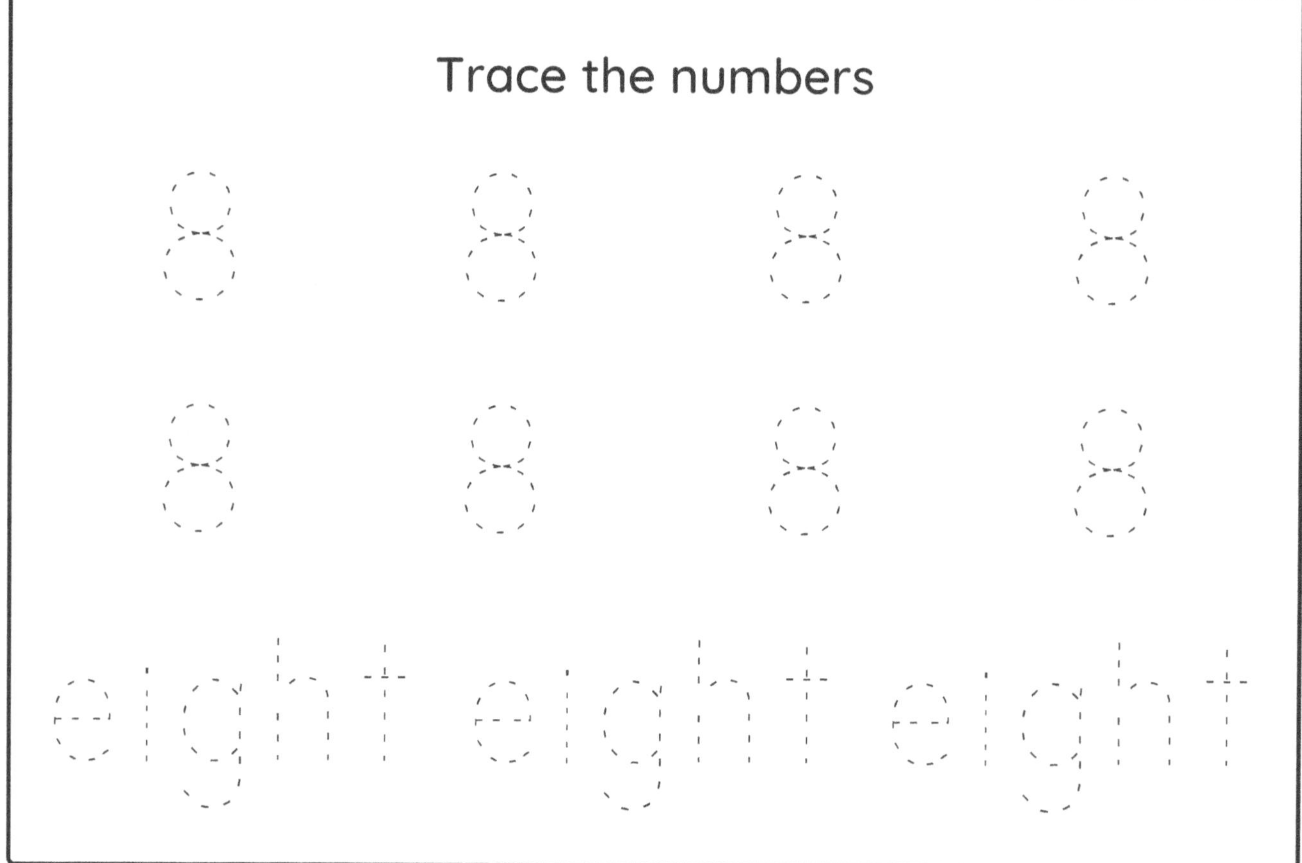

Trace the numbers

COUNT **AND** TRACE

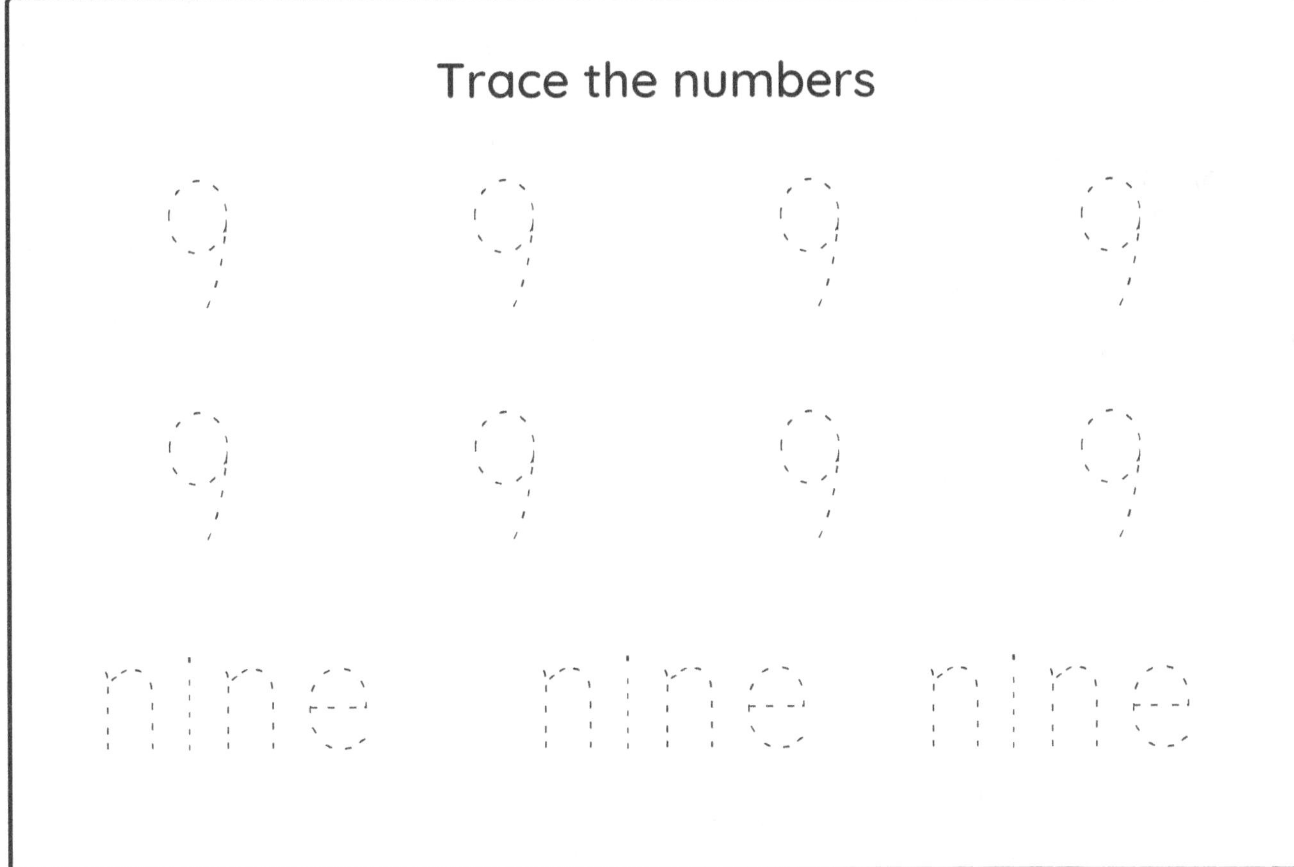

COUNT AND TRACE
0-100

zero

0

one

1

two

2 2 2 2 2

2 2 2 2 2

2 2 2 2 2

three

3 3 3 3 3

3 3 3 3 3

3 3 3 3 3

COUNT AND TRACE
0-100

four

five

COUNT AND TRACE
0-100

six

seven

COUNT AND TRACE
0-100

eight

8

nine

9

ten

10 10 10 10 10
10 10 10 10
10 10 10 10 10

eleven

11 11 11 11 11
11 11 11 11
11 11 11 11 11

twelve

12 12 12 12 12

12 12 12 12

12 12 12 12

thirteen

13 13 13 13 13

13 13 13 13

13 13 13 13

fourteen

14 14 14 14
14 14 14 14
14 14 14 14

fifteen

15 15 15 15
15 15 15 15
15 15 15 15

sixteen

16 16 16 16 16
16 16 16 16
16 16 16 16

seventeen

17 17 17 17 17
17 17 17 17
17 17 17 17

COUNT AND TRACE
0-100

eighteen

18 18 18 18 18

18 18 18 18 18

18 18 18 18 18

nineteen

19 19 19 19 19

19 19 19 19 19

19 19 19 19 19

twenty

20 20 20 20 20
20 20 20 20 20
20 20 20 20 20

twenty one

21 21 21 21 21
21 21 21 21 21
21 21 21 21 21

twenty two

22

twenty three

23

twenty four

24

twenty five

25

twenty six

26

twenty seven

27

twenty eight

28

twenty nine

29

thirty
30

thirty one
31

thirty two

32

thirty three

33

thirty four

34

thirty five

35

thirty six

36

thirty seven

37

thirty eight

38

thirty nine

39

forty

40

forty one

41

forty two

42

forty three

43

forty four

44

forty five

45

forty six

46 46 46 46
46 46 46 46
46 46 46 46

forty seven

47 47 47 47
47 47 47 47
47 47 47 47

forty eight

48 48 48 48 48

48 48 48 48 48

48 48 48 48 48

forty nine

49 49 49 49 49

49 49 49 49 49

49 49 49 49 49

fifty

50 50 50 50 50
50 50 50 50 50
50 50 50 50 50

fifty one

51 51 51 51 51
51 51 51 51 51
51 51 51 51 51

fifty two

52 52 52 52 52
52 52 52 52
52 52 52 52

fifty three

53 53 53 53 53
53 53 53 53
53 53 53 53

fifty four

54

fifty five

55

fifty six

56 56 56 56 56
56 56 56 56 56
56 56 56 56 56

fifty seven

57 57 57 57 57
57 57 57 57 57
57 57 57 57 57

fifty eight

58

fifty nine

59

sixty

60

sixty one

61

sixty two

62

sixty three

63

sixty four

64

sixty five

65

sixty six

66

sixty seven

67

sixty eight

68

sixty nine

69

seventy

70

seventy one

71

seventy two

72

seventy three

73

seventy four

74

seventy five

75

seventy six

76 76 76 76 76
76 76 76 76 76
76 76 76 76 76

seventy seven

77 77 77 77 77
77 77 77 77 77
77 77 77 77 77

seventy eight

78 78 78 78 78 78 78
78 78 78 78 78 78 78
78 78 78 78 78 78 78

seventy nine

79 79 79 79 79 79 79
79 79 79 79 79 79 79
79 79 79 79 79 79 79

eighty

80

eighty one

81

eighty two

82 82 82 82 82 82
82 82 82 82 82
82 82 82 82 82

eighty three

83 83 83 83 83 83
83 83 83 83 83
83 83 83 83 83

COUNT AND TRACE
0-100

eighty four

84

eighty five

85

COUNT AND TRACE
0-100

eighty six

86 86 86 86 86
86 86 86 86 86
86 86 86 86 86

eighty seven

87 87 87 87 87
87 87 87 87 87
87 87 87 87 87

eighty eight

88

eighty nine

89

ninety

90

ninety one

91

ninety two

92

ninety three

93

ninety four

94 94 94 94 94 94
94 94 94 94 94 94
94 94 94 94 94 94

ninety five

95 95 95 95 95 95
95 95 95 95 95 95
95 95 95 95 95 95

ninety six

96

ninety seven

97

ninety eight

98

ninety nine

99

one hundred

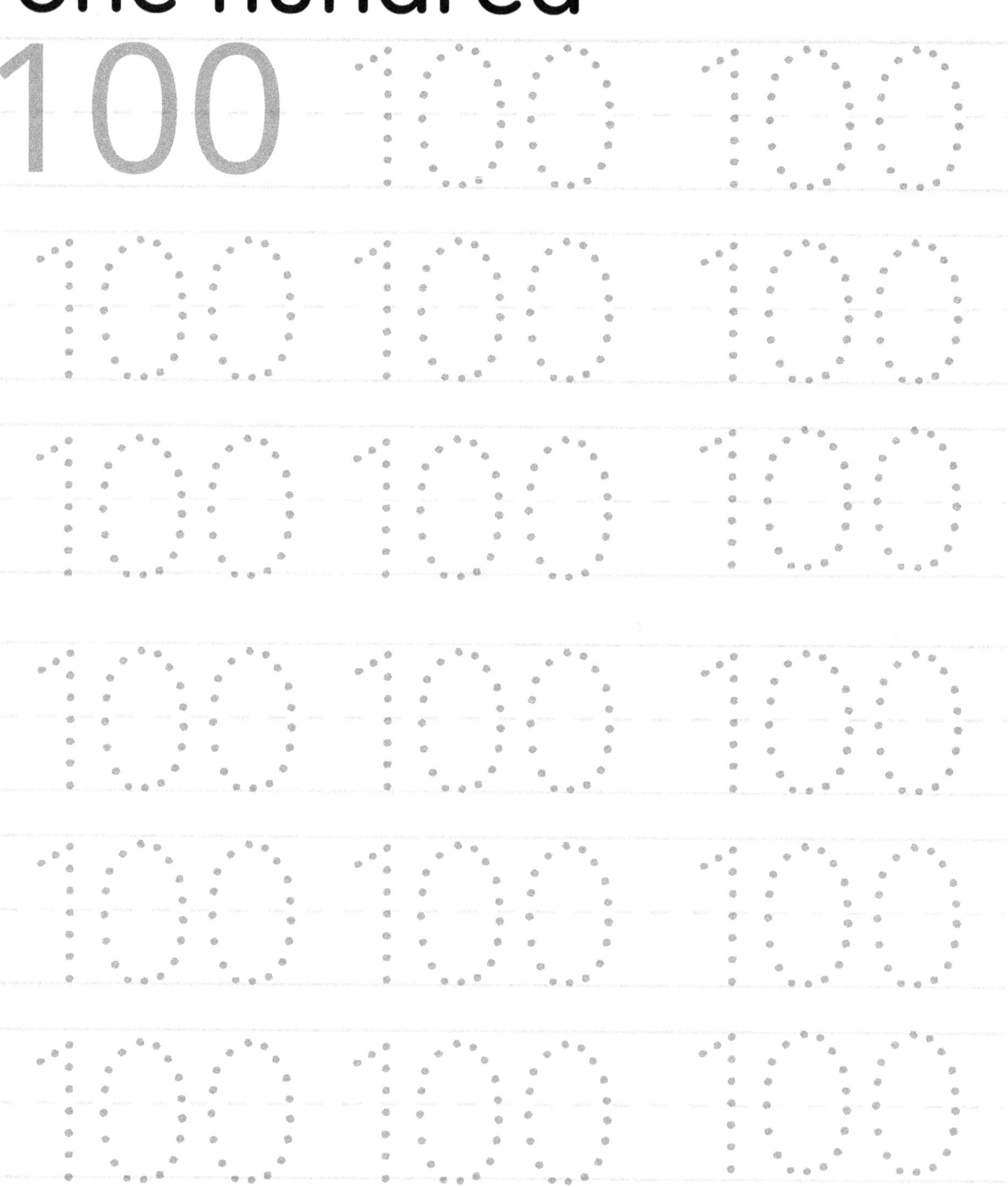

ONE

TWO
2

THREE
3

4
FOUR

5

FIVE

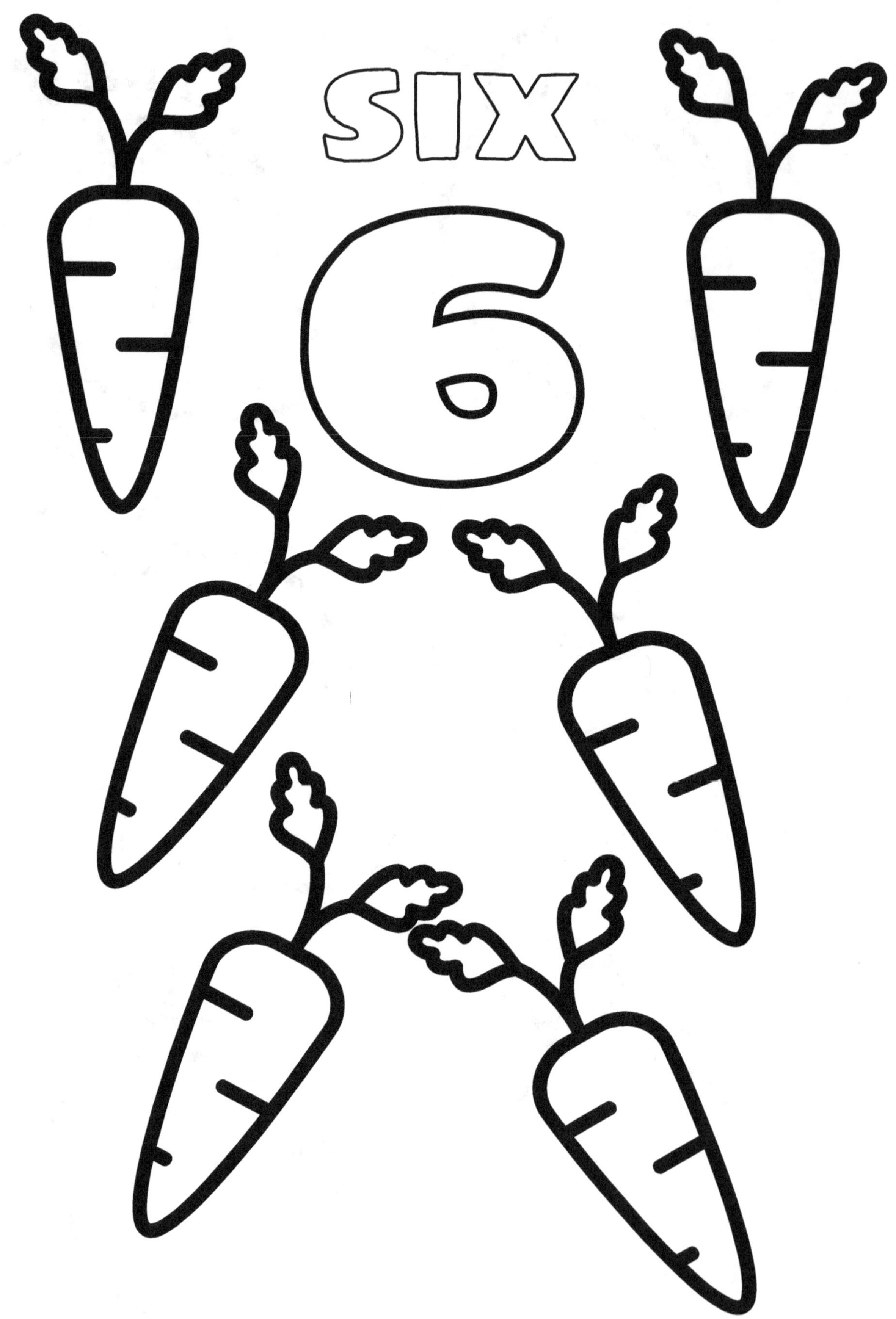

SIX
6

7
SEVEN

8
EIGHT

NINE
9

FIND THE MISSING NUMBER

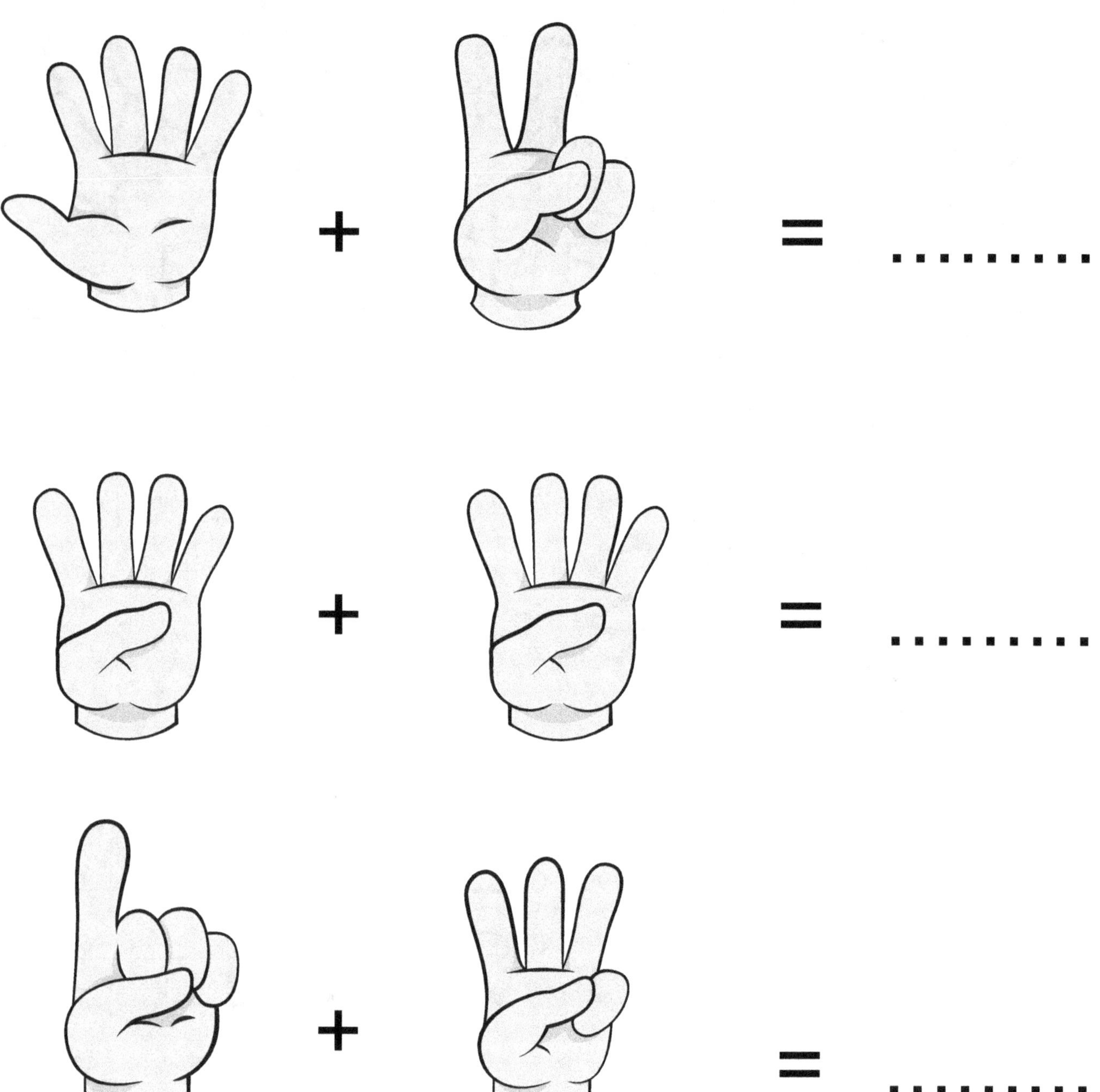

FIND THE MISSING NUMBER

 - 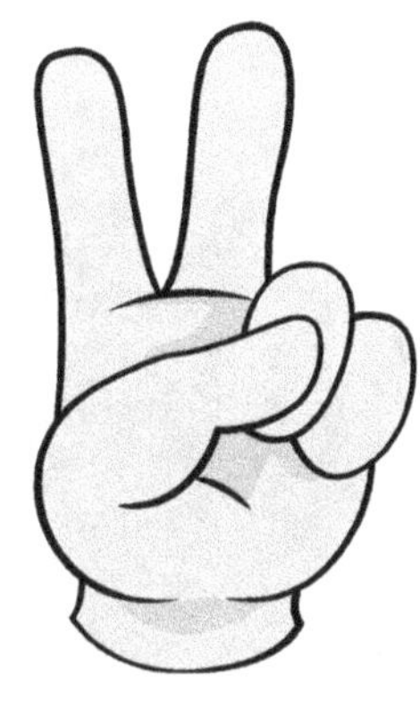 = 

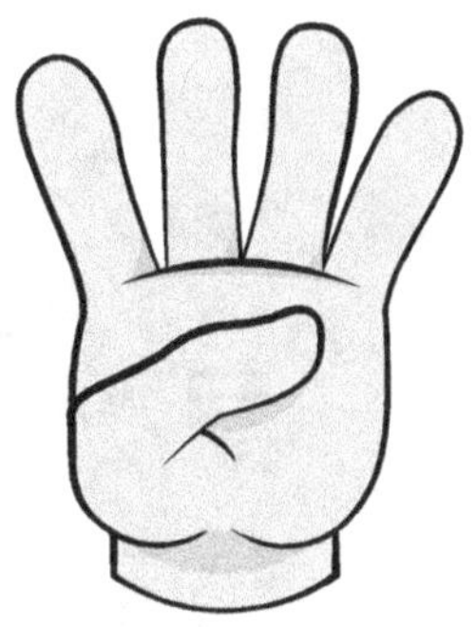 - 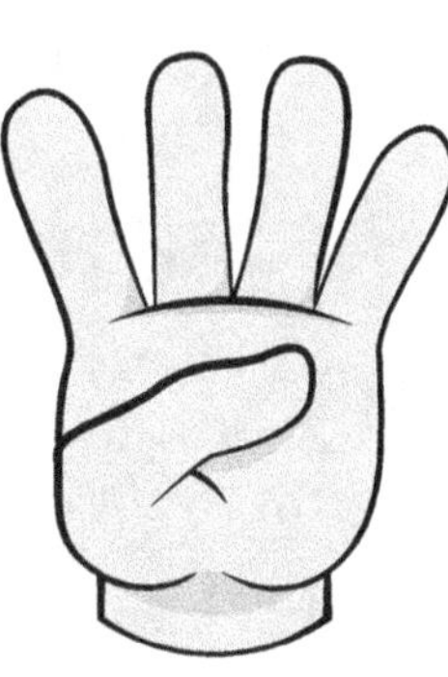 = ...

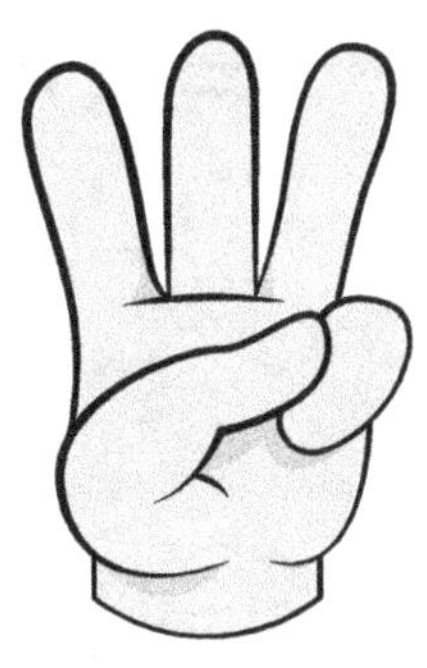 - 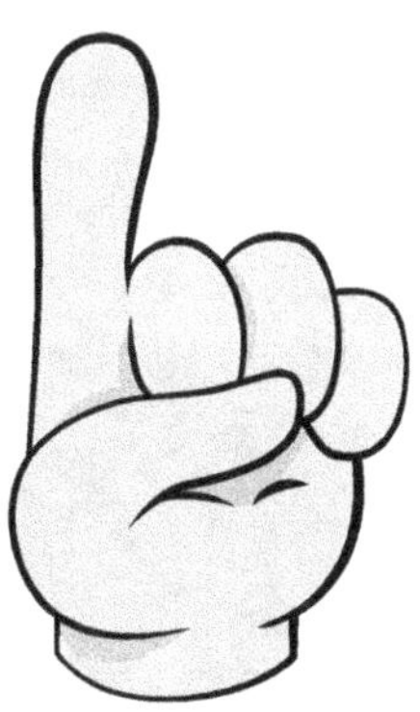 = ...

FIND THE MISSING NUMBER

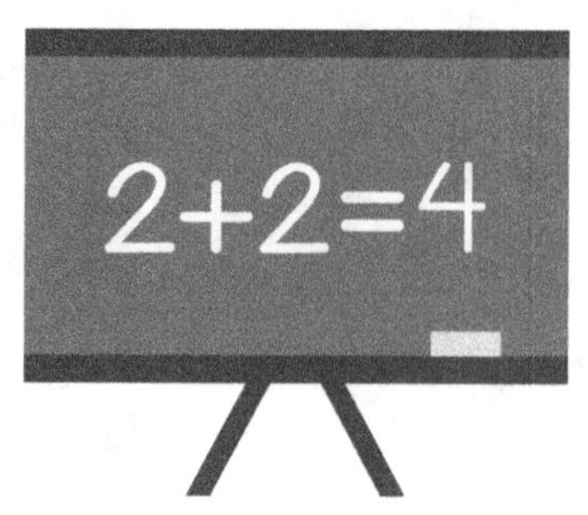

5 + _____ = 5   1 + _____ = 1

9 + _____ = 18   7 + _____ = 11

10 + _____ = 20   3 + _____ = 35

5 + _____ = 6   9 + _____ = 30

50 + _____ = 100   16 + _____ = 59

FIND THE MISSING NUMBER

5 - _____ = 5   2 - _____ = 1

9 - _____ = 1   6 - _____ = 2

10 - _____ = 20   3 - _____ = 33

5 - _____ = 25   15 - _____ = 30

50 - _____ = 50   19 - _____ = 19

SMALL FISH, BIG FISH

BIG FISH: **SMALL FISH:**

MATH MATCHING GAME

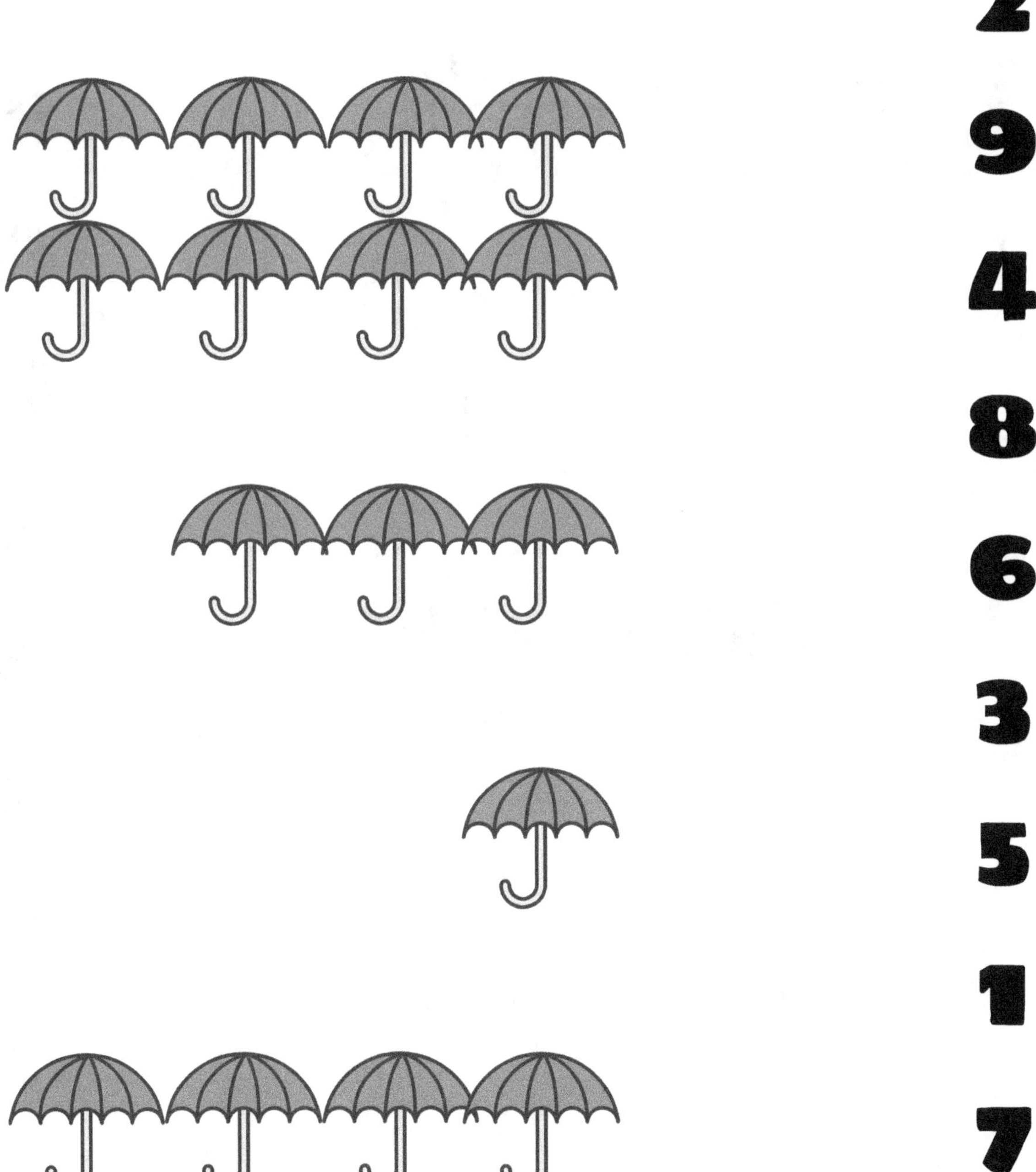

2
9
4
8
6
3
5
1
7

MATH MATCHING GAME

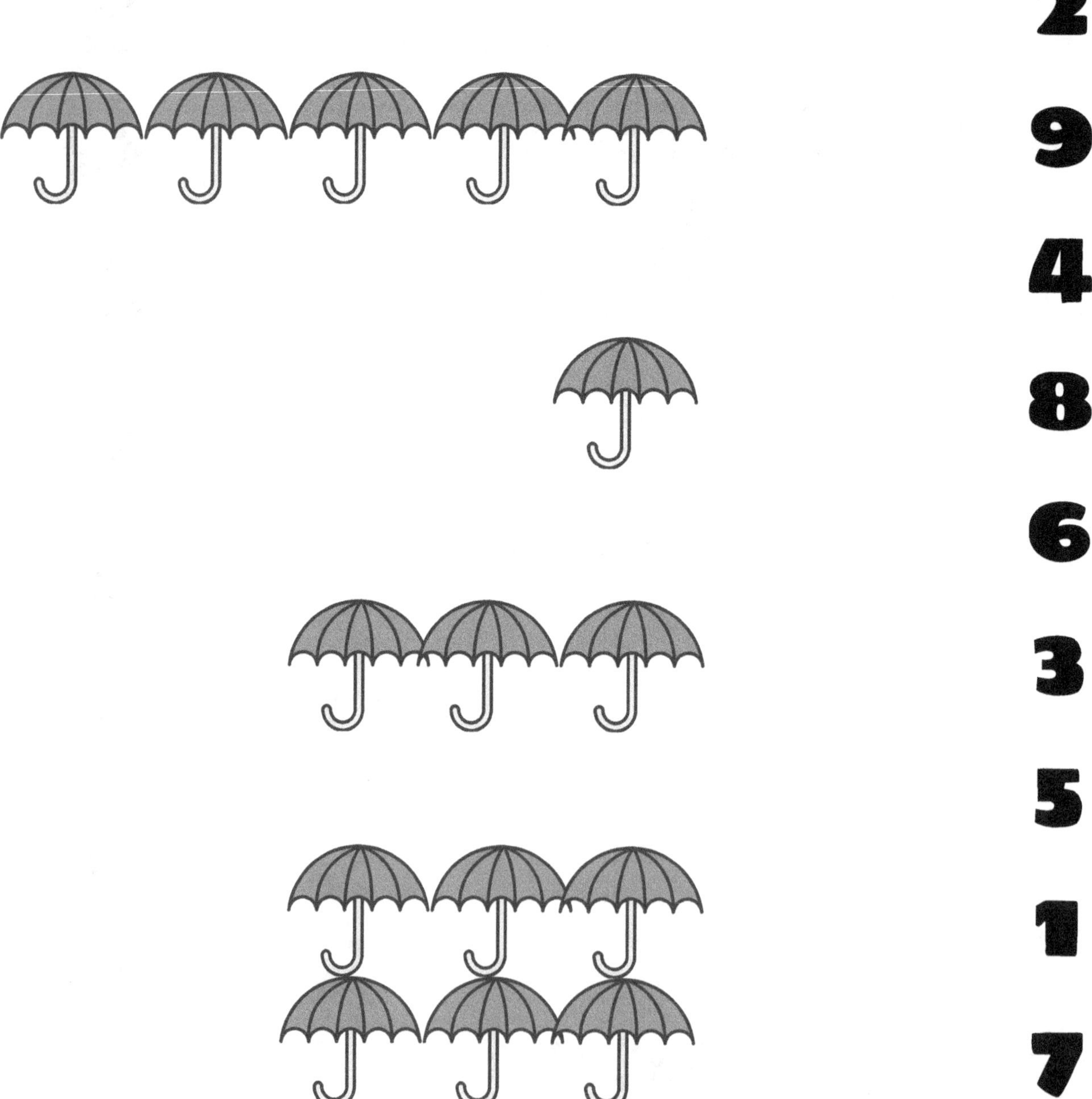

2
9
4
8
6
3
5
1
7

MATH DICE GAME

ADD THE NUMBERS THAT ARE ON TOP OF THE TWO DICE AND WRITE THE CORRESPONDING SUM ON THE BLANKS.

MATH DICE GAME

Add the numbers that are on top of the two dice and write the
corresponding sum on the blanks.

MATH DICE GAME

Add the numbers that are on top of the two dice and write the
corresponding sum on the blanks.

MATH DICE GAME

Add the numbers that are on top of the two dice and write the corresponding sum on the blanks.

ROCKET MATH

Solve the equations to launch the rockets!

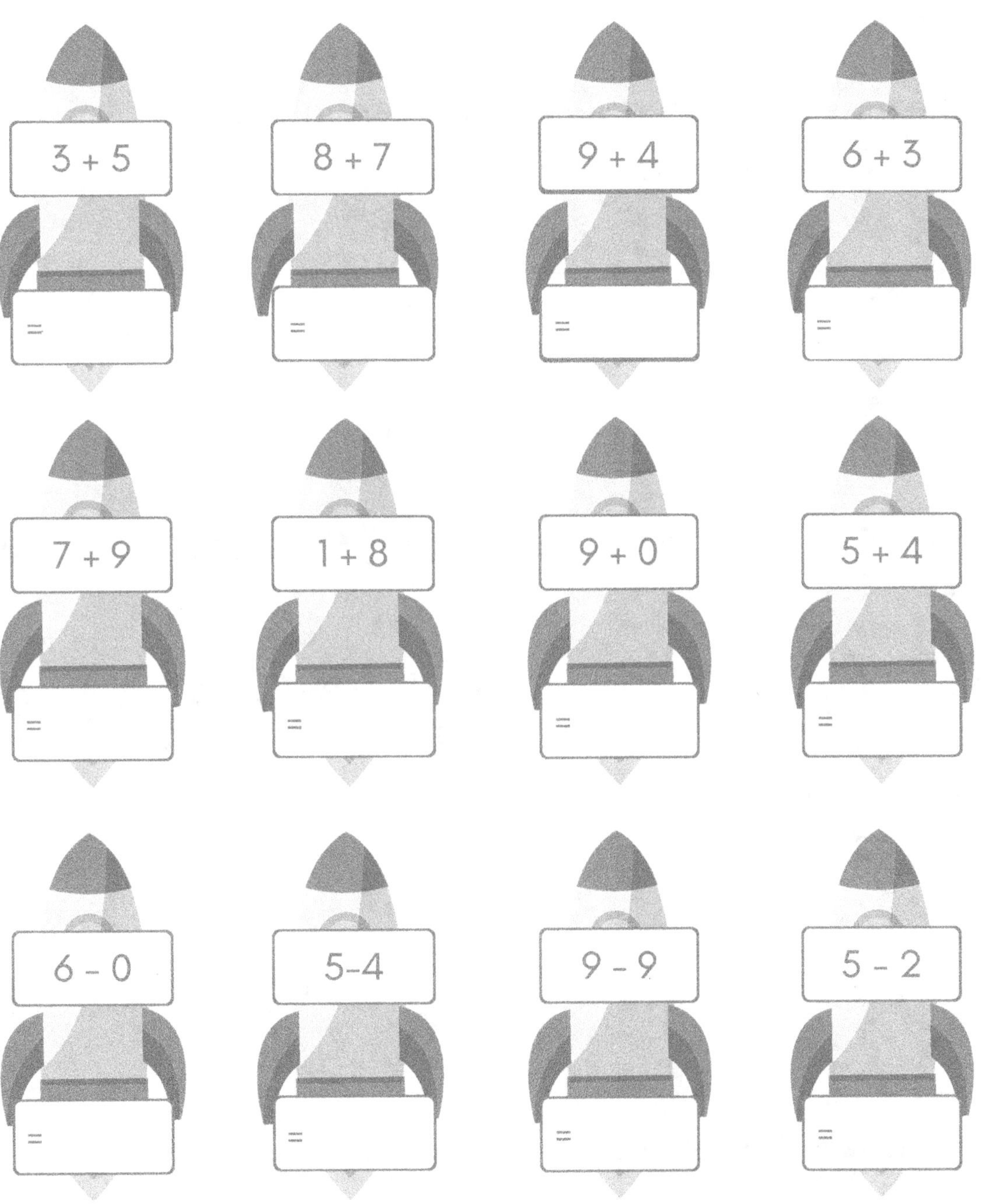

The Counting Game

Fill in the missing numbers as you count from 1 to 100

1	2	3	___	5	6	7	8	9	___
11	12	___	14	___	16	17	18	___	20
21	___	___	___	___	___	27	28	29	30
___	32	___	___	35	___	___	___	39	40
___	42	___	44	___	46	47	48	49	50

The Counting Game

Fill in the missing numbers as you count from 1 to 100

51	52	53	___	55	56	___	58	59	___
61	62	___	64	___	___	67	68	___	70
71	___	___	___	___	___	77	78	79	80
___	82	___	___	85	___	___	___	89	90
___	92	___	94	___	96	97	98	99	___

CLOCK

Fill in the missing numbers and coloring

All About Shapes

Trace and color in the shapes below.

TRACE THE LETTERS

Aa Bb Cc Dd Ee

Ff Gg Hh Ii Jj Kk

Ll Mm Nn Oo Pp

Qq Rr Ss Tt Uu

Vv Ww Xx Yy Zz